Wintertime Rhymes

Season's Greetings

Edited By Donna Samworth

First published in Great Britain in 2017 by:

☙ Young**Writers**

Young Writers
Coltsfoot Drive
Peterborough
PE2 9BF
Telephone: 01733 890066
Website: www.youngwriters.co.uk

All Rights Reserved
Book Design by Ali Smith
© Copyright Contributors 2017
SB ISBN 978-1-78820-592-4
Printed and bound in the UK by BookPrintingUK
Website: www.bookprintinguk.com
YB0314C

Foreword

Dear Reader,

Welcome to Wintertime Rhymes, a showcase for our nation's most brilliant young poets to share what they love most about winter and the festive season. From poems about Christmas and snow to drinking hot chocolate in front of the fire, this collection covers every aspect of wintertime.

Young Writers was established in 1991 to nurture creativity in our children and young adults, to give them an interest in poetry and an outlet to express themselves. Seeing their work in print will encourage them to keep writing as they grow and become our poets of tomorrow.

Selecting the poems has been challenging and immensely rewarding. The effort and imagination invested by these young writers makes their poems a pleasure to enjoy reading time and time again. I hope you enjoy reading them as much as we did.

Donna Samworth

Contents

Independent Entries

Waqas Hayat (18)	1
Jasmine Lowen (14)	2
Anna Maria MacDougall-Smith (16)	4
Asvitha Sarma (11)	6
Pari Kathuria (12)	8
Sofia Madelaine Zervou	10
Eva Harriet Haynes (10)	12
Ellie Crowson-Jeffery (16)	14
Taslima Khanom (12)	16
Amanda Troncoso-Morales (10)	18
Feby Babu (13)	20
Harnie Thiyohupillai (13)	21
Alvi Shams	22
Taylor Kelly Munro (16)	23
Hannah Forster	24
Mackenzie McGeown-Lambert (13)	26
Ella Colbourn (12)	27
Eleanor Guthrie (15)	28
Youmna Adel Mahmoud Hasanin (12)	30
Maariyah Daud (11)	32
Summerpreet Kaur (13)	33
Aysha Siddiqa Rahman (11)	34
Kiaya Lawson (15)	36
Abdur-Raheem Modan (15)	37
Rachel Daly (11)	38
Imaan Mohammed (14)	40
Summer Cuviello	41
Sebastian Hall (12)	42
Adarsh Ram Sivakumar (10)	44
Syeda Mashaim Bukhari (13)	46
Ned Hasson (10)	47
Eleanor Newman (11)	48
Sarah Faraz (11)	50
Parnika Jawalkar	51
Daijah Valentine (14)	52
Kaartika Chitturi (12)	53
Anna Haslam	54
Ashani Gunaseelan (12)	55
Armaan Mohammed (14)	56
Emily Bradley (11)	57
Olajumoke Esther Badiah	58
Courtney Sedgbeer-Hatton (13)	59
Soha Borouni (14)	60
Ishani Devi Aggarwal (8)	61
Yaana Mishra (10)	62
Sara Ahmed (14)	63
Alaha Baig	64
Luke Sheldon	65
Amelia Hines	66
Skye Morley (10)	67
Hannah Pinfield-Wells	68
Abdullah Mahdi Syed (12)	69

Beehive Preparatory School, Ilford

Faaris Malik (10)	70
Yash Patel (10)	71
Zayba Umar (10)	72
Eashan Patel (10)	73
Shivam Gupta (10)	74
Tiana Gunputh (11)	75
Kajanantis Skandamoorthy (11)	76
Sulaiman Ahmed (10)	77

Belswains Primary School, Hemel Hempstead

Robert Turculet (10)	78
Jessica Cox (9)	79
Ava Rose Lehner (9)	80
Sereena Rooney (10)	81
Isabelle Anne Lehner (9)	82
Leo Snelgar (9)	83
Paula Forcada Mata (9)	84
Mark Chapman (10)	85
Nicole Lall (10)	86
Mikayla Maule (10)	87
Viktorija Starovoitova (10)	88

Brackley CE Junior School, Brackley

Anais Huggins (11)	89
Sophie Woodward (10)	90

Christ Church CE Primary School, Birmingham

Bareerah Farooq Janbaz (8)	91
Ahlam Mohamed (9)	92
Tasneem Omar (9)	93
Hassaan Khan (8)	94
Emaan Karim (8)	95
Suheila Arten (8)	96
Yasmeen Saleh (8)	97
Aleesa Maryam (9)	98
Haytham Abdorahman (8)	99
Saba Saghir (9)	100
Sumayyah Mahbub (9)	101
Adam Khan (8)	102
Muath Hunaiber (8)	103
Maariyah Nadim (8)	104
Zheer Omer (8)	105
Rahmah Mohammed (8)	106
Fatima Jamil (9)	107
Najma Suleiman (9)	108
Abdul Rahim (8)	109
Sulaiman Khan (9)	110
Laraib Akram (8)	111
Kitty Kaur (8)	112
Hassan Arshad Hassanili Khan (9)	113
Maleeha Rashid (8)	114

Highshore School

Runnel Hilarion (12)	115
Baffour Bediako	116
Bradley Fenn	117
Josiah Ferguson (16)	118
Caroline Jacobs (13)	119
Victor Adeniyi (18)	120
Rebecca Legood	121
Takudzwa Masamba (12)	122
Harry Lorraine-Grimes (12)	123
Lilli Stockham (11)	124
David Pearson (12)	125

Holy Trinity CE Primary & Nursery School, Richmond

Frankie Durham (10)	126
Salma Mohamed Abdelbaky (9)	127
Georgia Allbut (9)	128
Alek Pniewski (9)	129
Maddy McGeoch (10)	130
James Howe (10)	131
Panka Eszenyi (9)	132

Oakridge Junior School, Basingstoke

Gierome Ezekiel Inguito Tinga (8)	133
Aarib Mohammed (8)	134
Bethany Binder Gharu (9)	136
Ben Cameron (8)	137
Deshane Hemmings (9)	138
Kyla Howlett (9)	139
Ruby Bailey McCarthy (9)	140
Sasha Suzanne Joyce Petchey (9)	141

Felicity Hepden-Barker (9)	142
Rhiannon Dixon (9)	143
Erin Langford (8)	144
Jacob-Joshua Agozzino (8)	145
Nivedha Sudhakaran (8)	146
Mollie Lovick (9)	147
Samuel Ackland (9)	148
Alexandra Kalashnikova (8)	149
Fida Salam (9)	150
Adonia Bala (9)	151
Rosie Livingstone (8)	152
Malak Oisti (9)	153
Robert Allwright (8)	154
Ella-Mae Stent (8)	155
Jack Williams (8)	156
Sreeram Suresh Setlur (8)	157
Ollie Cowton (8)	158
Kia Crawford-Hicks (9)	159
Isabelle Pauline Pike (9)	160
Adam Grant (8)	161
Poppy Williams (8)	162
Cindy Tafrey (9)	163
Charlotte Hazel Fry (8)	164
Harris Waheed (8)	165
Ronnie Tuffs (8)	166
Sam Thorpe (8)	167
Cameron Reeve (8)	168
Loren Carter (8)	169
Marnie Clarkson (9)	170
Krishna Volety (8)	171
Rose Mason (8)	172
Misha Sirnani (8)	173
Jacob Newson (9)	174
Tyson Mathurin (8)	175
George Chubb (8)	176

Peak Forest CE Primary School, Buxton

India Page (9)	177
Callum (10)	178
Ethan White (8)	179
Grace Kirkham (10)	180

Matthew Jagger (8)	181
Bethany Hadfield (9)	182
Beatrix (10)	183
James G (8)	184
Oliver (9)	185
Jim Hayes (7)	186
Maia Fletcher (7)	187

The Manor Academy, Mansfield

Michaela Hancock (14)	188

Ysgol Gynradd Gymraeg Llantrisant, Pontyclun

Megan Jenkins (11)	190
Nia Powell (10)	192
Hedd Teifi (10)	194
Harley Rose Vigliotta (11)	195
Llewelyn Gwynne (10)	196
Emily Lauren Gait (10)	197
Emily Harris (9)	198
Grace Morgan (9)	199
Mali Foster (9)	200
Mali Stevenson (10)	201
Owain Prys Ifans Jones (9)	202
Cerys Hulse (11)	203
Benjamin Samuel Williams (10)	204
Owain John (11)	205
Elis Burton (11)	206
Lili Hopkins (10)	207
Emily Amos (10)	208
Sam Jones (10)	209
Rhys Morgan Stephens (10)	210
Lois James (9)	211
Charlotte Simcock (10)	212
Jac Lloyd Lockett (10)	213

The Poems

Winter Nights...

What is this feeling within my heart;
Concealed by daylight hours, in a shroud of taut restraint.
Winter evenings consume, yesterdays pursue me,
Smiling, speaking, acting - I can cope, I can cope...
An injured heart bares healing in the nearness of love,
Yet love becomes frigid when winter sweeps in, I am alone.
The world is cold, my heart laments in fearful silence
Winter, winter, where are your friends?
Betrayed by the sheath of night, rejoicing in decay
In scornful silence, reflecting on unfulfilled dreams,
Dreading the night, enduring the day. Winter.

Hopes and dreams, rest upon a cradle of love,
Unconditional, fruitful, forbearing, eternal,
Winter steals, freezes, and denies.
To be alone in this season, is to be alone,
No voices, no echoes, no gentle memories shared.
A solitary tree yielding to an unfeeling winter,
Surrendering its leaves to winter's steel sky.
Fleeting sunshine, stolen, lacking kindness, or warmth
Sheets of invasive rain, such unforgiving indifference
Winter is reconciliation without forgiveness
Yet, it is the door to spring, and the resurrection of hope.

Waqas Hayat (18)

Life Is Cold

What is in a five-bird roast? I never know.
My aunt does, for sure, on Christmas Day
For her it's almost a rite of passage.
Myself, I prefer a gammon.
More succulent and tender.
Oh, what would it mean to be kissed? Under the mistletoe.
With bells, and holly, and tins of empty wrappers -
My brother, of course, eats the lot without shame.
I tell you this, but why do you care?
We've grown up now.

Do you ever miss me, I ask? Since you left.
For me it'll never be the same, this Christmas Day -
Greeting cards scream merriment,
But myself, I must mourn
And stare pensively out at the snow.
I am grown now.

Are you outside right now? It looks cold.
Perhaps you have a husband, this Christmas Day -
And you're kissing not far away,
Maybe for him, you're the gift he always wanted.
Maybe you're singing.

Are the trees bare where you are? I feel cold.
And do you remember that time, on that Christmas Day -
We were infinite. You were stunning in your fake Santa robes.

Red as holly, white like snow.
Are we grown now?

And note how you jumped out of my gift wrapping that day?
I am cold.
The choirs were lovely, but my eyes were yours -
You were like an angel, my darling,
But now I must weep.
You are gone now.

And remember the charity work? We are cold.
You were always giving to those around you
And we ate soup with the homeless and looked up at the stars,
Golden and bright
But you're gone now.

Do your lips still turn red and chapped? Life is cold.
I hope you know you're the best thing this Christmas Day.
Better than snowflakes and pies, and all the reindeer.
So my gift to you? My heart.
It's beating for you anyway.

Jasmine Lowen (14)

The Unseen

The storms blow,
Terrible wind and snow,
Ice covers the ground.
Nuts brought by the pound,
Fires in the chimneys,
Gatherings of families.

December has finally come...

Gifts wrapped up all neat,
Branches swaying to the beat,
Of Christmas tales,
And ice-skating fails.
Children out screaming,
With decorations already streaming.

December has finally come...

Perky adults bustle about,
Each over-buying without a doubt,
All feeling the Christmas spirit,
Candles meekly lit.
Children waiting for the day,
Presents already, under trees, lay.

December has finally come...

Scrooges curse and scowl,
Such a day so fair but foul,

Rejecting any and all cheer,
And at young people they leer.
Winds ripping their icy hearts,
And each hostile like rats.

December has finally come...

Wintertime in its youth,
But to some winter they loathe,
Out in freezing winds,
And facing winter sins.
Each night they lay outside,
With no one to confide,
Homeless to the bone,
Their only heat a piece of foam.

December has finally come...

So this Christmas year,
Think of the poor and here.
Please donate clothes and food,
And try and lift their mood.
The chill and sadness overcome,
December has finally come...

For Christmas is about giving,
Not receiving.

Anna Maria MacDougall-Smith (16)

Winter Wonderland

Outside in a winter wonderland,
The towering trees stand in a blanket of snow.
Mounds of pure-pearl snow, piles on the frosted ground,
It crunches like crispy leaves, that have been blown away with autumn.

Outside in a winter wonderland,
Icy fog hugs the chilly air.
Icicles, that are knives, are dotted here and there,
Glistening in the winter sunlight, which is a paradise.

Outside in a winter wonderland,
A cold, crisp crust of clean, clear ice settles on a solitary pond.
Thin ice spreads its arms around the pond,
An incautious step will make a crack.

Cold and chilly;
Freezing and frosty;
Icy and ice-capped;
Glacial and gelid;

But it is cosy, comfortable and comfy inside the house.
Snuggled up like a hibernating bunny,
Wrapped up tight as the blanket huddles you to a warm sleep.
A burning fire crackling as the heat flies towards you to soothe you,

A mug of hot chocolate is sitting next to you, smiling and waiting to be drunk.

Fire is extinguished so there's only a deafening silence,
Peaceful and quiet.
The sky is a deep-blue ocean,
With bright stars painted on.
The stars are valuable diamonds,
Just like the winter wonderland.

Asvitha Sarma (11)

The Pigs Pigalicious

Old Granny Pigalicious,
Who looked juicy and delicious,
Was sitting by the fire,
And warming up her toes.

Outside it was snowing,
And the layers were slowly growing,
But all the bugs were fine,
Huddled by Granny's toes.

Old Grandpa Pigalicious,
Who didn't look too delicious,
Was rummaging through the cupboard,
Oh where did it go?
He was looking for his blower,
His high-tech snow blower,
So he could create a path,
Through the many layers of snow.

The parents Pigalicious,
Who looked better than delicious,
Were scanning through the list of names,
For theatre shows and plays.
Then suddenly they found one,
The one they'd wanted to see,
They booked their tickets quickly,
As happy as could be!

The twins Pigalicious,
Who looked fine but not delicious,
Were donning all their winter clothes,
'Cause out they wanted to go!
They skated on the frozen pond,
Laughing all the way,
And built their yearly snowman,
Oh what a lovely day!

Now I'm going to tell you,
That this is my family,
This is what we do in winter times,
My family and me!

Pari Kathuria (12)

Magic Is In The Air

When you wake up in the morning, all tucked up in your bed,
With a red nose and joyful thoughts
Running through your head,
To open your curtains and find the grass caked in white,
And little children laughing, having a snowball fight.

To dream of that night that your stocking will be filled,
To try and spot the reindeer from a frosty window sill,
When you sit down on the sofa,
A cup of cocoa in your hands,
And hear the harmonies of the carol singers,
Like a private band.

And once you've stepped outside onto snow that is so soft,
You can hear your family
Collecting decorations from the loft,
As the smell of scented candles
Wafts through the winter breeze,
You struggle to open the frozen door with your golden keys.

Just thinking of all those presents
Sat under a tree full of light,
Makes you excited and ready for that magical night.

Winter is so special - full of magic you never knew,
You'd never think of the flying reindeer,
They're there but very few,

So if you don't believe in Christmas, you're missing out,
But the magic is still there without a doubt.

Sofia Madelaine Zervou

A Wartime Christmas

Once I went off to war
Felt like an apple without a core
Had no choice or I'd have to pay
Scared that this will be my last day

Leaving my family
With many tears
This was one of my greatest fears
I knew that this day would come
Sadness fills the hearts of love

In the trenches I shall wait
Hoping that we are not too late
As the Germans might start shooting
Waiting for the trumpets to start tooting

Me and my friend ran ahead
But within seconds he was dead
Fell on my knees filled with sorrow
Knowing his spirit shall always be hollow

Staying strong I carried on
Felt like I had done very wrong
Maybe I should have stepped in front
But I noticed that my sword was blunt

Then a bomb came from above
Saying my prayers to my loves
Then all over I saw red
Then I realised that I was nearly dead

Doctors came over and cleared the blood
Lifting me up out of the mud
No more beds for me to spare
Felt like I was lying in the air

As my eyes closed I screeched for help
Then I felt the urge to yelp
In my leg was an injection
Only just realising I had an infection

All the doctors ran away
Knowing it was not okay
I knew this was my last day
There on the floor I lay.

Eva Harriet Haynes (10)

Familiar Winter

Harsh backbite of the season's change,
Filling the air with heady smells of concave leaves crumbling,
Perhaps a futile glimpse of each year's death; or happiness that we're nearing the end,
But always coming, always falling, always stepping.

Stepping into the slippers of a time that came before,
Brushing the skeletons off your jacket with frostbitten fingers,
Closing two freezing eyes and setting your bag by the door,
The warmth of a hug, blankets of comfort from a pair of happy arms.

Arms well known yet long since seen,
Ones known from flickers of a past gone but easily recalled,
Melting even the coolest of the ice that seems so uncontrollable,
Bringing back the dregs of summer still caught in your family's eyes.

Eyes watching from trees covered in caress of the sky,
Waiting for the familiar laugh and love,
Such a thing always known,
Protecting from snowfall and angry blasts of ice.

Ice-cold glasses filled brimful of childlike wonder,
Christmas pudding wishes with the burn of adulthood,
Teaching to be young again without stress or worry,
Before spreading your tongue to the sky to taste memories
on your lips.

Ellie Crowson-Jeffery (16)

Winter

Winter is the time of year,
Where we all get out our cosy gear,
'Cause soon it's gonna get really cold,
And none of us really need our mother's scold.

Winter is the kind of sign,
For all to have a gathering kind,
And catch up on things we've missed,
As life's too short to not attend and take the risk.

Winter is the season where,
My favourite weather seems to care,
And come out once, do its chore,
To shower us with snowflakes and more.

Winter is a great excuse,
To be let out of school and run off on the loose,
Instead of being tortured by teachers,
To be spoiled by other winter creatures.

Winter is the time when smiles are seen most,
Whether people are making Christmas toasts
Or finally having time to create reminiscences,
As those are your life's eminences.

Winter is when we end an old chapter,
To begin a new one, that others flatter,
And be filled with hope for the coming seasons,
Where joy and laughter awaits for whatever reason.

Taslima Khanom (12)

Christmas Around The World

A Christmas TV programme
Watch the villain scram
This is Denmark reporting
Time to do some transporting.

Santa's translation is 'Christmas goat'
The fishermen are home in their boats
Santa lives in the Northland
Here is Finland.

Wreaths of red, green and gold
But it's not too cold
This is Argentina
Now let's go to Bosnia.

Bosnia doesn't do Christmas
Now let's go some distance
To a small Piccadilly
All the way to Chile.

Lots of barbecues
High up in the blues
Tons of Christmas lights
Just enjoy those sights.

The Japanese eat fried chicken
KFC needs to quicken
Couples eat at a restaurant
There's no time to be gaunt.

Silent Night is Stille Nacht
But it's actually packed
Be ready for a sternsinger
German children are prone to linger.

This is Egypt
Filled with peaches
It's not 25th December
It's on Jan the 7th, remember.

The Basque country has a magical man
Called Olentzero, with a big tummy span
His tale may be dreary
But he's always cheery.

Amanda Troncoso-Morales (10)

Winter Is Finally Here

Winter is finally here
The warmth of summer has completely disappeared
Roads have become blanketed with thick layers of snow
Preventing workers from reaching their workplaces
And preventing school-goers from being able to go
For children this is great
No school, snow and an early break
Delays and cancellations continue across the city
Many starting to shake their heads in self-pity
Meanwhile
Others choose to stay inside
Cosy in front of a warm, open fire
And when Christmas finally arrives
With family and friends gathered on December twenty-five
Wearing Christmas jumpers and full of good cheer
Thankful to have been able to make it here
There are celebrations made and carols sung
And delicious food suitable for everyone
Huddled around the TV till dawn's first light
Grateful for a fabulous Christmas night
Seeing many smiling and having a great time
Makes me appreciate how much I love these things
About wintertime.

Feby Babu (13)

Awaiting For Christmas

Tree leaves wet and brown
'Just wait for the sky to frown.'
Countless snowmen abducting our innocent little town
My little sister as Mary in the nativity, foraging for a gown.

Commonly, an army of weightless morning dew would fall to suffocate the greenery below
But nearing Christmas means we have to welcome the Mellow fleet of snow.
The prosperity begins when a child's eyes dart over to the window
When their head is still relaxed on a pillow.

Even through the coldness of some's misery
Many still view Christmas as their biggest treasury.
'Hot chocolate anyone... with marshmallows and cream!'
Outside, the festive magic will cause an ordinary mouth to produce enchanting steam.

The last of the jubilant decorations has been placed
And the beautiful star on top gleams.
Feeling the urge to be on Santa's nice list
We hurry to bed early commanding sweet dreams.

Including me and you,
Many still view Christmas as their biggest treasury too...

Harnie Thiyohupillai (13)

The White Blankets Of Winter

Everywhere there are white blankets of snow
Now is the time when the cold wind will blow
This is the time when there is lots of fog
I sit down by the fire and drink hot chocolate from my mug

Snow hanging majestically from trees
People climbing mountains to ski
The leaves fall and give the snow some space
Everyone who is skiing is having a race!

You can go sledging on the highest mountain tops
I go so fast and feel like I'm going to drop!
Even if I'm on the highest mountain peak
All the beautiful snowflakes are unique

I'm making a snowman with my friends
It is like the fun will never end!
Whilst making the amazing snowman
Suddenly a big snowball fight began!

But when that time comes when you start to see the sun
Sadly it is time to end the fun
The snowman melts and to me that seems like a tear
I hug him and say, 'See you next year!'

Alvi Shams

Christmas Time

Christmas time comes around once a year,
we fill a room full of laughter and cheers.
Although we love our families constantly,
we only show them through special occasions which is quite sad actually.
We see the joy on our little sister's face
as she opens her presents and her wish becomes a reality.
The atmosphere is calm as the white snow trickles down the window,
the light breeze which gazes on our neck sends shivers down our spine,
this lets us know that it's Christmas time.
We gather around the fireplace with the lit-up tree set amid the sparkling room.
The stockings will dance slowly to the calming music which will surround us.
Later on, we will gather around the dinner table where the food will be exquisite. Christmas time is the place to make everlasting memories
and it will always be something we will never want to leave...

Taylor Kelly Munro (16)

Christmas Eve

Bare trees and bitter cold,
Grey sky and there is no snow,
But still we laugh,
And still we play,
Waiting to see Santa's sleigh.

My little sister's face lights up,
When upon our door there is a knock,
Is it Santa?
Has he come?
But no it is just our mum.

'If you do not go to sleep soon,
Saint Nick won't come up to our house,
So close your eyes,
Close them tight,
And believe in Christmas with all your might.'

'What if he doesn't come?'
My little sister asks me sadly.
Have you been good?
Have you been nice?
Remember, he has checked it twice.

Then she lay down upon her bed,
After wishing me a merry tomorrow,
I closed the curtains,
I turned off the light,

And fell asleep as quick as light.

Then the next day my sister woke me up,
We went down the stairs two at a time
'He has been!
Yes he has been!'
And there were more presents than I had ever seen.

Hannah Forster

Winter Joy

Winter joy is inside everyone,
The way the snow falls while we sit by the fire,
A time to celebrate and have some fun
And to hear the singing from a choir.

Winter is a thing to remember,
But it is not just a time in December!
It is a day of family and love
To celebrate the friendship with the gift of turtle doves.

I love this time of the year
From the moment the snow arrives
This time creates lots of memories
And lots of things to make and do for the tree's accessories.

The best part is Christmas,
A time where families come together,
And where people give and believe,
Christmas is a gift that anyone can receive.

Winter is not just a season
It comes with a variety of holidays,
That everyone can enjoy but mostly, this season creates
Winter joy all around.

Mackenzie McGeown-Lambert (13)

Winter Solstice

Standing by the window
I see winter's shy afternoon light fading, unnoticed
Leaving dusk in its place.
In the distance, rows of spindly branches fringe the fields
Their weak arms stretching as they search for the sun.

On the horizon
Lies a sliver of hope,
The last fading memory of the day,
Soon to be enveloped by ink-stained skies.
A floundering cloud hides from winter,
Taking refuge from its bullying grasp.

Outside my window
The lone lamp post no longer spies on my street.
Winking, it apologises for the ever-growing darkness
Hiding the start of frost ferns that will
Cement themselves to my window sill.

In the sky
A victorious, swollen moon illuminates the bitter blackness,
Surveying its wintry kingdom.
The battle is won.
This is winter's time now.

Ella Colbourn (12)

Varnished Branches

The stormy north sends driving forth,
The blinding sleet and snow.
Snowdrops varnish branches white,
As frosted white winds blow.

The sky falls dark as dusk draws in,
Streetlamps flicker in the night.
Stars appear from behind the black,
Shining oh so bright.

Smoke drifts lazily from the chimney,
Across the freezing cold night sky.
Christmas lights flood the streets,
Illuminating snowflakes as they fly.

Logs burn gently in the fireplace,
Crackling as they glow.
Sparks dance before my eyes,
Swaying to and fro.

Icicles hang down from the gutter,
Great glossy shards of ice.
Candles burning in the doorway,
Orange and mixed spice.

Carollers at the doorstep,
Angelic hymns they sing.
Church bells in the distance,
Join in as they ring.

Now night falls upon us,
And everything is still.
Yet the flurry of snow continues,
Landing on the window sill.

Eleanor Guthrie (15)

Seasons Change

Our clothes become arranged
Packed in different sizes and shapes
Our wishes exchanged
Yet we remain unchanged
Despite the weather that may surround us
We still enjoy the quiet meaningless discussions at night
As sparks shine bright outside

We all hold our warm cups
Laughing our lives away
Drunk on the happiness
That seems to be radiating off of us in big waves

Snow starts to embrace our buildings and gardens
iPads and iPods are forgotten,
Children's eyes go wide
They run outside
Guided by their own imagination
They begin to craft and create
Showcasing their hidden talents

What can you wish for
While the wind roars
There's nothing better
Than seeing these children
In their jumpers and sweaters
Celebrating their own holidays and festivals

We all come together
To laugh and smile
Because winter has this special magic in it
And you can't help but admit.

Youmna Adel Mahmoud Hasanin (12)

Winter Winter You've Come Here Again

Winter winter you've come here again
The last time you came I was ten
Remember that time we played in the snow
We built a snowman and went with the flow

Winter winter you've come here again
The last time you came I was ten
Remember that time we had a snow fight
O just remember it was a wonderful sight

Winter winter you've come here again
The last time you came I was ten
Remember that time we were shivering and shaking inside
While it was snowing swiftly outside

Winter winter you've come here again
The last time you came I was ten
Remember that time we opened my present
And looked inside to find something pleasant

Winter winter you've come here again
The last time you came I was ten
Remember that time we were around the Christmas tree
O that was such a glee

Winter winter you've come here again
The last time you came I was ten.

Maariyah Daud (11)

Seasonal Joy

Piles of snow everywhere to be seen,
The joy of festivity living in my brain.
Me singing Ariana Grande Christmas songs
And feeling the Christmas spirit all around

I've been down this round before
Blinded by craziness of the seasonal joy
Winter is a seasonal joy because...
Billions of lights are blinking
And everybody's singing 'I love Christmas'

No reason to forget this joy
So we will keep the sleigh bells ringing
And the timeless thoughts of the wonder season

But the snow clinging to the trees won't always be there
Because as the sun wavers
The frost will fall soundlessly to the ground.

So live up every minute of the wondrous days
And enjoy the frosty days of the seasonal joy.

Summerpreet Kaur (13)

Winter Dreams

Speckles of white dust velvets my window,
As I snuggle up, while I hear a crescendo,
Of a mere snowball game!

My heart lifts with light at the sight of snowmen,
Children prancing, hands frozen...
With fun!

How I longed to go there myself,
Digging a graceful snow angel, or even an elf!
However, my snow-locked house won't let me...

Merry voices sing,
While sliding down cliffs with magical snowboards, swinging...
Off icicles!

Grandpa says this is the last snowy winter...

I stand, the wind blowing my icy hair.
How would I cope if Grandpa was right!
Winter? Oh, winter. It would be like a faded memory!

Snowflakes blind my eyes,
I need to stop my winter from saying goodbye -
I just need to, need to, need to!

I carry out my quest,
Not a single winter whisper,
Lest I...
Forget winter and move on!

Aysha Siddiqa Rahman (11)

Alone At Christmas

He was alone on a cold winter's night,
Not a decoration or card in sight,
Waiting for the solitary season
To pass, his heart hurt for one sad reason,
Since her passing he could not quite enjoy
Christmas like he had when he was a boy,
Once upon a time they put up the tree
Together but now he couldn't quite see,
The worth in creating a reminder,
That he continued to live without her,
Christmas songs only made him remember
Her smile, her warmth, her love of December,
And now as the month passed with him alone,
It didn't quite have the same happy tone,
Gingerbread left his tongue tasting bitter,
He began to hate the sight of glitter,
They caused him to miss her all the more,
The lovely woman he had fallen for,
The festive season only caused him pain,
He wouldn't miss Christmas if it never happened again.

Kiaya Lawson (15)

Winter's Verse

When December comes:
Coats and jumpers thrust hastily on
Every toe and finger numbs
As we are finally awoken from summer's hellish slumber

Hellish, that's what I said; you'll be surprised to hear
I love winter, and hate the sun.
The cold, to me, is very dear
But winter has become somewhat less magical of late

For snow no longer falls
Global warming's doing, no doubt.
But still the over-zealous malls
Rant about sales and Christmas time.

I do love winter (a sentiment sometimes met with jeers)
I love home, being blanketed with a mug of hot chocolate to hand
It is the cooling calm in the storm of years.
Watching films and reading novels.

It is what keeps mankind from
The foreboding doom that threatens us all
It is our salvation, our fight song.
So long live the mighty cold!

Abdur-Raheem Modan (15)

You know,
The one about what I like
About winter,
I just don't know where
To start

I know I like the presents under
The tree,
I know I like the stockings by
The bed,
But that's what everyone's gonna be
Writing about

I could do the frost outside on an
Early morning,
I could do the warming
Roast dinner,
I like those but that's not
Quite right

I need something just
Really special,
Maybe the shimmering decorations,
Wait, no,
Maybe when it's dark really early,
Not that

I will write that poem soon,
Don't worry,
It won't ever be
Too late,
Just one more brainstorm,
Or two

My favourite thing about
Winter is
The snow and when I get to build
A snowman,
So I think I'll write about that and
The rest.

Rachel Daly (11)

Steamy Winter

The cold takes over and I freeze like ice,

From my bed I do not rise,
Scarves and hats bob around the streets
Like they have a life of their own,
Yet with friends, a way to survive is shown.

The days grow shorter,
And a parent with a licence becomes your very own porter,
Snowflakes from the sky
Gently descend to the tip of tongues,
But, all is forgotten when sitting there
And coughing out are your lungs.

The only good thing about winter
Is that you're one step closer to spring,
And you finally get to stroke the tip of a bird's wing,
And the flowers on a tree bloom,
You get to see the sun
And wave goodbye to the long winter of doom.

Imaan Mohammed (14)

Frozen Waters

When darkness falls for the winter,
Bare branches of trees enhanced with crystalline icicles.
In the cascade of gentle snowflakes,
Penguins go on a waddling parade.

Polar bears wade in frozen waters;
These powerful, white bears searching for food supplies.
Wolves howl and snicker through the gloom of the winter air.
Deep within the frigid aqua waters,
There is a pod of black and white orcas.
Seal pups start to play in the glistening snow.

From a dusting of flakes to a sparkling white blanket;
These animals disguise themselves in the winter solstice.
Arctic foxes scamper in blizzards like frosty blurs.
The northern lights painted in the jet black sky;
Pastel night of rare beauty as earth's gleaming wonder.

Summer Cuviello

Foggy Heath

I dawdled in my running kit
I shivered in my timber
I saw frosty buoys bobble up and down
On a freezing lake.

This had been done before
But only in a different season
When I saw birds
Tall trees.

But I saw very little
Because of the fog
I saw the grim brown meadows
Lacking proper nature.

I came to the place
That was normally Smiley's
But now in the coldness
Moscow rules.

I was chilled to the flesh
And my body parts failed
As we left the hairpin
My feet were on gravel.

But my heart warmed
To think of good Nero
A perfect morning
A winter's day.

Sebastian Hall (12)

Winter Effects

Winter comes after fall,
Night comes fast and dark,
Lights are always on,
So much darkness to overcome!

Winter comes as a monster,
With so much chillness,
With boiling heaters,
Fireplaces raging,
So much heating to come!

Winter comes as Christmas gift,
With so many presents,
And yummy food to eat,
So many wishes to come!

Winter comes as a white blanket,
With snow of course,
And new friends called snowmen,
So much fun to come!

Winter comes as a new year,
So many greetings and celebrations,
With new aspirations and desires,
So much happiness to come!

Winter comes before spring,
Waiting for flowers in every lane,
Every tree desiring for leaves,
So many colours to come!

Adarsh Ram Sivakumar (10)

Watching Winter

Countless, maze-like angels obliquely descend.
Autumn is finally coming to an end.

Unclad trees, alpine mountains and vivid green grass
All draped with a cavernous white veil.
Babbling, burbling, bounding the azure stream
Now frozen like a fairy tale.

Winter's gale whining wind makes leaves dance
And sends spirits soaring.
The sombre grey clouds are clamorously snoring.

Effervescent adolescents frolicking in the snow.
Sledding in it, throwing it and moulding it like dough.

My breath is fogging up the icy windowpane
As I watch this buoyant scene,
Knowing that anon everything will be green.

Syeda Mashaim Bukhari (13)

The Cold Heart Of Winter

The sky lashes out with bitter wind,
The trees beg for mercy,
Death stalks the rolling hills,
As storms patrol the country.

Darkening clouds kidnap the sun,
The land grieves and moans,
The hissing rain calls for decimation,
The frozen lake groans.

Darkness battles the sunlit hours,
The light of day restricted,
The country, under shadow, cowers,
Before the damage inflicted.

Empty skeletons coat the hillside,
The remains of fallen trees,
Winter's wrath will not subside,
'Til nothing but terror he sees.

His cold heart is one of stone,
His mind a reckless monster,
His feelings are for himself alone,
For he, he is Winter.

Ned Hasson (10)

Christmas Catastrophe

Is it a book?
Is it a clown?
Is it a rabbit that jumps up and down?

It gives you that thrill,
Just to see,
The bulging presents under the tree.

You think you know,
You can't be sure,
What presents lie in store.

On Christmas Day,
Oh my it's a dismay!
Not what you were hoping for today.

You sigh,
Try to be pleased,
But you can't help being peeved.

You think to yourself,
This can't be,
My present under the Christmas tree?

The present won't change,
However much you stare,
Life isn't fair.

Oh well you say,
Without a tear,
Perhaps I'll get it next year?

Eleanor Newman (11)

A Winter's Night

The sky is dark,
The ground is white,
The world is peaceful on this winter's night.

Not from the trees, a call of a bird,
No one around, not a sound to be heard.
Can't hear a laugh, a car, nor a mouse,
Scurrying across the floor in the house.

Everyone snuggled in their cosy beds,
Floating away slowly, slowly.
I feel like a cloud drifting in the air, dreaming, dreaming.

I suddenly wake up,
I hear the sweet sound of sparrows singing,
The wind howling,
The trees swaying,
And thunder crackling.

I smile inside, I feel free!

Sarah Faraz (11)

Dear Santa

I needed to write a poem
For my boring, tedious homework
(Though, I don't really see the point)
As it takes up all my time and hard work...

Dear Santa,
For Christmas I would like:
Three million bottles of Fanta
And an Apollo mountain bike.

I also want,
The world's nicest aunt.
A golden iPad Air,
And to be elected as mayor.

The biggest hippopotamus,
And a juggling walrus.
A dancing, entertaining clown,
And the Queen's precious crown.

A reindeer for Christmas,
And maybe a circus.
A lovely happy elf,
Who is always willing to help.
Especially with my homework,
As it takes up all my time and hard work!

Parnika Jawalkar

Mysterious Animal

Winter days the forecast must be
Snow and rain
But that doesn't distract me
I'm looking for an animal

An animal that is forgotten
Left to hibernate in the snow
But helps keep the world spinning
That's what nobody knows
I'm looking in the snowy trees
And behind the snowmen
Where is this creature hiding?
That's what I would like to know.

Deep in the forest is a place no human goes
A place where nature and wildlife can grow
It's hidden beneath the mist and snow
That is the place where this fantastic creature goes.

Daijah Valentine (14)

A Homeless Winter Experience

Whilst the snow was falling down and down
I walked along the frosty ground
The white grass crunched as I stepped on it
And my footsteps printed neatly amongst the blades

As I paced through the chilly pathway
I heard Christmas carols being sung
And felt the warmth of the fire crackling in the hearth
I admired the gorgeous Christmas trees,
Decorated with sparkly Christmas ornaments

I wished I had a home and a family
I wished I could celebrate the splendour of Christmas
I wished I enjoyed the magnificence of winter
I wished all of these wishes should come true
Only they won't, they never did...

Kaartika Chitturi (12)

Christmas

Christmas is a time when we come together,
For memories we are sure to remember.
To assure people sweet and tender,
How wonderful it is that Christ is our Lord and saviour.
Let love be in your heart,
As Christmas unites those who have drifted apart.
We will cherish Christmas forever,
As we dance and celebrate together.
Christmas is a time for giving and receiving,
That's why Christmas isn't worth leaving.
The church bells ring,
As people sing,
The joy that Jesus brings,
Just how Christmas is meant to be,
For me.

Anna Haslam

The Christmas Holidays

It's Christmas time again,
A time for family and friends
Oh when will it snow, when?
I wrote a letter to Santa wanting some gel pens!

It's a time for Christmas cheer,
Christmas Day is really near.
This is the festive year,
Santa will come with all his reindeer!

Now it's time to go to sleep,
Remember leave some mince pie for Santa.
Reindeer elegantly leap, while you sleep,
No milk? Don't worry just give Santa some Fanta!

It's Christmas Day,
It's time to be on our way.
It's also the Christmas holidays,
It's Christmas! Hip hip hooray!

Ashani Gunaseelan (12)

Yet Another Christmas Story

The snow awaits December
Awaits December to fall
To fall and to bring smiles
Can you imagine such a beautiful sight?
The kids playing and creating snow angels
The adults sitting around the embers and sipping tea
The naked trees clothed by snow
That didn't quite make it to the ground
Snowflakes floating onto my tongue as gracefully as swans
If only I had a wand
I would make it snow every day
This beautiful memory would be reality
Winter wonderland, before my eyes
Every day and every night...

Armaan Mohammed (14)

Nine Things I Love About Christmas

I love that fresh smell of pine on our sitting room floor,
The thick green wreath that adorns our wooden door.
I love the crunch of the snow that our warm winter boots make,
The way we all sigh when clearing the snow makes our backs ache.
I love the jingle of bells on our green elf hats,
The way that the ice confuses the cats.
I love the shopping for clothes and lots of other treats,
The way I tear open my stocking to find packs of sweets.
I love that hush! As I try hard to fall into a sleep...

Oh dear, if Santa comes, I'd better not peep!

Emily Bradley (11)

Christmas Is Near

Everyone knows that Christmas is nearby
When Santa's reindeer fly in the night's sky
I just can't wait to see what Santa brought for me
Especially for my family
Everybody come join our Christmas this year
And don't forget your family cheer
As he flies around going over seas
He places presents under trees
As Christmas decorations shine very bright
We sing carols every night
All our hearts shine bright light
All our hearts join together
As we sing songs all together.

Olajumoke Esther Badiah

A White Christmas

Just as the cold winter's day was dawning,
I was awoken by the sound of sleigh bells in the morning.
I ran outside only to find snow on the glistening floor,
I put on my shoes and coat and ran out through the door.
Twisting and turning the snow was falling.
Children were singing and sleigh bells were ringing.
The smell of spices,
Lingered through the air,
Reaching my nose, oh so cold and bare.
A white Christmas is all I asked,
My wish has finally come true at last.

Courtney Sedgbeer-Hatton (13)

Dear Santa

There are many questions I'd like to ask,
Like have you ever been drunk or put on a cucumber mask?
Have you ever been to a swimming pool or been to a park
Or have you ever played Monopoly or played hide-and-seek in the dark?
Have you ever felt like it all gets too much
Like what if you forget to bring Australia's presents or one of the reindeer hold a grudge.
Have you been caught by news reporters or fans
Or been to places like Winter Wonderland?
Who will be the next Santa Claus?
Will it be Mrs Claus?

Soha Borouni (14)

The Magic Of Winter

Dancing snowflakes falling in the night, while the graceful ice skaters twirl in the moonlight,
Carols are being sung while decorations are being hung.
The beautiful big tree stands tall and proud,
Children run around it and shout out loud!
Christmas time has everyone in a good mood,
There is always hot chocolate, cupcakes and yummy food!
The best bit about Christmas is when I finally get to see, what presents Santa has left for me!
It is truly a magical time of year, as everyone is full of Christmas cheer.

Ishani Devi Aggarwal (8)

Winter

Snowflakes flying across the sky
Girls and boys admiringly looking up high,

Footprints printed across the ground
Carols making a lovely sound,

Skies are looking very pale
It seems like a fairy tale,

Steam entering through the chimney
Everybody snuggling up happily,

Santa and his elves on their way
A sack filled up with toys to play,

Bold trees standing firmly
Clouds making your sight hazy,

The weather is turning colder
Have a merry and happy winter.

Yaana Mishra (10)

Winter Is Here!

When the rain pours down onto Earth, it calms me.
I am no longer crying alone.
When the wind roars past us,
Demolishing everything in sight, it brings peace upon me.
I am no longer the only thing being destroyed.
When the snow and ice pile on to all surfaces,
Freezing them stiff,
It makes me one with the universe.
My mind isn't the only cold, dark holder of abolishment.
When winter arrives, the darkness within me bursts out,
I camouflage.
Then, I disappear.

Sara Ahmed (14)

Winter Wonderland

The ice glows bright just like starlight,
Snowflakes dance around,
Soft footprints on the floor crushing away the moist pearls,
Fairy lights dangle from every corner,
Swaying about with the wind
'Ho, ho, ho!' cries out a voice,
Landing swiftly with a click,
I glance around without a sound and there stood an old man wearing a red waistcoat,
Presents? Presents! Yeah!
We thank him for the gifts and return home with burning smiles.

Alaha Baig

Winter Forest

The top of the trees,
Embracing the crisp, cold air,
Drifts huddle below.

A still morning air,
Effortlessly flows through the leaves,
Enshrouded in ice.

Ice melts into glass,
Refracting the fragile rays;
Secrets of beauty.

A porcelain moon,
Engulfs the forest in a
Tranquil, peaceful light.

Luke Sheldon

December Magic

Mince pies on a plate
Lovely cold milk on a coaster
Ready for this special date

Running up the stairs at the speed of lightning
Filled up with joy
Nothing frightening

Tucked up in bed
Snug as a bug
Followed with a kiss on the head

Sleeping quietly with no sound
Secretly excited
For Santa to come round

Magic in the air
Spread around
With love and care.

Amelia Hines

Fog

Creeping in,
Silently,
Like a mysterious dream,
Or swiftly moving clouds.

Running now,
Thick as snow,
Creepy and eerie,
Fresh and cold.

Where does it come from?
Why is it here?
It doesn't exactly raise Christmas cheer!

Dull and horrid,
Hard to see through,
Ugh.
Fog.

Skye Morley (10)

Winter

Snowflakes fall,
We buy anti-freeze from a stall.
We open presents,
We eat a pheasant.
Santa eats the mince pie,
He also wears an Xmas tie.
We watch the Queen's speech,
We want to eat the last candy cane on the tree
But we can't reach it.

Hannah Pinfield-Wells

Snow

Snow
Snow falling,
Drifting in the wind,
Touches the ground,
A gentle blanket,
To cover the trees,
Through their loss of leaves,
Warming them up,
Before they melt away,
For spring.

Abdullah Mahdi Syed (12)

The Old Man

He lay on the grass of snow,
Looking at the snowflakes falling below,
He saw people ice skating in the rink,
And he remembered the time
When he was young
And taken to the ice rink.

He drove home and his car was frozen,
He came back to children
Wanting some toys and snow fights,
He was wearing a jumper covered with snow
And a garden covered with white glimmering ice and snow.

The children asked him
If they could put some cookies and milk next to the fire,
The Christmas tree was glowing
From all the lights around it,
They were shining like an angel,
Which was hanging on the top of it.

Faaris Malik (10)
Beehive Preparatory School, Ilford

Winter

It's that time of year again,
It's now time to celebrate Christmas,
Open your presents
And spend wonderful time with your family.

Santa will come down your chimney,
Give you presents and ho, ho, ho,
The snowmen are being built,
And the children are having a jolly good time.

The squirrels are going to sleep
While we are up and lively,
It's Christmas time,
The time to be happy,
Let's all celebrate together.

Yash Patel (10)
Beehive Preparatory School, Ilford

Christmas

C hristmas, what a jolly day.
H aving time with family and friends.
R eindeer galloping in the snow.
I cy sculptures gathering around the ground.
S anta Claus saying, 'Ho, ho, ho, merry Christmas!'
T rees with decorations in houses.
M arvellous presents for children.
A ll the children singing songs.
S adly we have to say goodbye to Christmas until next year.

Zayba Umar (10)
Beehive Preparatory School, Ilford

Winter

It's that time of the year when people become happier.
It's like a firework lighting up and exploding inside.
Christmas lights are like a firework
Displayed on every household.
The snowflakes start to fall
As I stare out of the frosted window.
Hot chocolate waiting to be sipped
And gooey marshmallows waiting to be chewed.
This is the doing of the magic of winter,
This is winter, the doing of nature.

Eashan Patel (10)
Beehive Preparatory School, Ilford

Christmas

C hristmas is a time of fun and joy,
H appy old Santa is coming to town,
R eady little trees, it's not time to frown,
I t is time to settle down,
S o as the stars look down, no time to frown,
T rees that glow, trees that die,
M erry Christmas you and I,
A s others glow yours will shine,
S tars that stay top of the line.

Shivam Gupta (10)
Beehive Preparatory School, Ilford

Christmas Tree

The Christmas tree glowing
The golden star shining
The baubles twinkling
Hiding between the leaves flickering
Tinsel gleaming
Fairy lights glistening
Presents waiting to be opened
Bringing happy smiles to families
And finally one last wish from Santa
Wishing everyone a merry Christmas
Ho, ho, ho!

Tiana Gunputh (11)
Beehive Preparatory School, Ilford

Dusty Christmas

The way a crow
Shook down on me
The dust of snow
From a hemlock tree.

It's time for Santa Claus
To get his claws out
It's time to put up your tree
Santa's planning to give presents out
Be present on Christmas.

Merry Christmas.

Kajanantis Skandamoorthy (11)
Beehive Preparatory School, Ilford

Winter

W onderful winter breeze in the air
I nside it's warm, no coats must be worn
N ot a single summer flare
T he snow starts to fall as we stare
E verybody throwing a snowball
R eally rapidly the snow falls.

Sulaiman Ahmed (10)
Beehive Preparatory School, Ilford

A Street In Winter

The howling wind pierced through their spine,
A bitter wind took hold,
Everybody lit their fires
And escaped the numbing cold.

The disturbed snow bore recent marks
Of children that came to play,
Streets so icy and covered in frost
Caused vehicles to delay.

The winter's air turned liquid to ice,
Wherever water lay,
The weather got steadily colder,
Worsening every day.

The street lights towered over everyone's head,
Peering down below,
They towered above the city,
Emitting a pale glow.

There was a massive cheer when winter stopped,
Spring did not delay,
The weather was warm like an oven turned on
During March and April and May!

Robert Turculet (10)
Belswains Primary School, Hemel Hempstead

A Winter's Day

A blanket of snow covers the ground,
The cold, chilly air is all around.
A robin is sitting in his nest,
Showing off his vibrant red breast.

The heavy snow upon the trees,
As it falls it sets the branches free.
Trees glisten as you stare,
No leaves to be found as they are bare.

The icicles in the trees are as clear as glass,
Whereas the frost has covered the grass.
Trees begin to shiver and shake,
Down by the ice-topped frozen lake.

The snowflakes are gleaming in the sunlight,
They are twinkling jewels ever so bright,
As I walk along I hear no sound,
Except for the crunching snow on the ground.

Jessica Cox (9)
Belswains Primary School, Hemel Hempstead

Wintertime

Trees whisper to each other
As the wind makes their branches bare,
Even limbs shiver in the cold air.
It is winter!

Snowflakes come down, cautious not to make a sound,
Falling delicately to the ground.
It is winter!

There is a thick blanket of snow,
Nature is in a deep slumber below.
It is as soft as silk
And as white as milk.
It is winter!

Children have a snowball fight,
This is a delight.
It is winter!

Everyone goes inside to keep warm,
Before a cold begins to form.
It is winter!

Ava Rose Lehner (9)
Belswains Primary School, Hemel Hempstead

Winter Is When...

Winter is when...

The loud wind whistles
And when snow decorates
Bushes and thistles.

Winter is when...

The lake starts to freeze up
And when you can have hot chocolate
In a warming, large cup.

Winter is when...

Robins sing their morning song
Whilst lots of other animals join along.

Winter is when...

Our faces get tickled by the snow
And when the sun gives us a faint glow.

Sereena Rooney (10)
Belswains Primary School, Hemel Hempstead

Winter Warmth

The whistling wind brushes my cheek,
I see my breath as I speak.
Clothes hug me tight from the cold,
Winter is a season to behold!

Glistening snow drapes all that I see,
A robin starts to sing to me.
I stop and listen to his melody,
As he dances joyfully from tree to tree.

His chest is a glowing light,
It truly is a wondrous sight.
Warmth of feeling emanates like the robin's heart too,
As this winter warmth makes my heart thaw through.

Isabelle Anne Lehner (9)
Belswains Primary School, Hemel Hempstead

Winter Poem

The sun rose up, crisp and bright
To see the snow left by the night.

Through the snowflakes you could hear
A robin calling somewhere near.

The robin soared up in the sky
Through the clouds that were so high.

The sun went down like a candle dimming
Through the sky the clouds were swimming.

Leo Snelgar (9)
Belswains Primary School, Hemel Hempstead

A Winter Morning

In the lonely park
A tree covered by a frosty snow blanket
Watches over the icy lake.

The elegant bridge is reflected
In the crystalline lake
Which acts like an immense mirror.

The pale blue sky is whispering
To the fluffy clouds
While the wind whistles.

Paula Forcada Mata (9)
Belswains Primary School, Hemel Hempstead

My Dream Winter

I would hear birds sweetly singing in the distance
So very grateful for their existence
I would see the tree branches swaying
The soft snow with children laughing and playing
I would taste the soft snow melting in my mouth
Something you don't always experience down south!

Mark Chapman (10)
Belswains Primary School, Hemel Hempstead

Winter Wonders

As the evening fell and the darkness came
I could hear someone whispering my name.

The street lights winked at me in a weird way
But why did this happen? I wanted to stay.

The snow was twinkling in the moonlight
My heart was full of delight.

Nicole Lall (10)
Belswains Primary School, Hemel Hempstead

The Mysteries Of Winter

I would like to be sitting in the gleaming snow
As the snowflakes wink at me as they brightly glow
Thick sheets of snow would cover the ground
And other snowflakes would dance around
The snow would cover my feet across
And nature might hide but would not be lost.

Mikayla Maule (10)
Belswains Primary School, Hemel Hempstead

Freedom Of Sledging

It would be an exquisite moment
To glide along the winter's snow
On a yielding carpet feeling free
Intricate snowflakes kissing me
Tenderly, softly on my face
To be free is a wonderful place.

Viktorija Starovoitova (10)
Belswains Primary School, Hemel Hempstead

A Negative Type Of Christmas

Yay it's Christmas (not!)
I'm so excited for Christmas (not!)
It's overly happy, it's overly fun
Smiles pasted on the joyous faces of everyone.

The fire is roaring,
Carol singers' voices a-soaring,
I just want to send them crying,
To stop my ears from bleeding out and dying.

Too much money is wasted,
On turkey becoming basted.
I don't ask for much, just to be left alone,
In my heavily fortified, Christmas-proof home.

The snow as pure as a newborn babe,
Tickles my nose, it drives me insane!
The unique little patterns that dance around,
Make me want to crash them
And trample them on the ground.

But the presents, well they're not so bad,
At least they don't make me horrendously mad...

Anais Huggins (11)
Brackley CE Junior School, Brackley

Winter From Scrooge's Point Of View

It's time to migrate for winter is here,
Grr, I wish I could up sticks and disappear.
Let the snow fall, that's if we've got it here
While I'm in a bunker, away from my fear
Of sludgy rain and mould that dries
Oh such a joy: how time flies!
Can you see the sky go black?
Oh, and leave a mince pie for Santa with his sack
Shops can sell their bizarre range of gifts,
And people can shiver and hope for the weather to shift.
All this can happen, and much more,
But I'd rather be asleep - *snore, snore!*

Sophie Woodward (10)
Brackley CE Junior School, Brackley

I Love Winter!

I love winter!
Winter is cold.
It's the day Jesus Christ was born.
Celebrations are starting on Christmas morn.
Santa's coming, giving presents,
I tell you, it really is pleasant.
Loudly singing 'Jingle Bells'.
Smelling the sweet pudding's smell.
Look at all the falling snow.
It's all the spirit of Christmas you know.

Bareerah Farooq Janbaz (8)
Christ Church CE Primary School, Birmingham

Wonderful Winter Wonderland

I love winter's wintry cold.
Now it's time for the sun to go.
Bye-bye sunshine,
Bye-bye rain,
Welcome snow,
Let's celebrate.

Now there are short days,
More time to sleep,
Let's shop at Primark
And go to KFC.

Now it's ending, time to say goodbye.
Hope you enjoy this wintertime.

Ahlam Mohamed (9)
Christ Church CE Primary School, Birmingham

Winter Gifts

I love winter, winter is cold.
It's full of joy and that is what is told.
It's full of hot chocolate,
It's full of presents
And that's why Christmas is full of pleasures.
It's time for snowball fights,
It's time for fun
And that's what winter is
And that is done!

And that's why I love winter!

Tasneem Omar (9)
Christ Church CE Primary School, Birmingham

Winter

S now, snow, I love you,
N ow please don't go, I want to play.
O h Santa, why don't you play in winter?
W inter is the best season ever.
M r Santa, why do you have a long beard?
A ll the children in town are finding you.
N ight-night Santa, why do you come in the night?

Hassaan Khan (8)
Christ Church CE Primary School, Birmingham

Snowmen Take Over Christmas!

S nowmen are fun to build.
N othing else is better than a snowman.
O n the ice skating rink, people dance with them.
W onder why they do that?
M en always eat the snowman's nose.
E ating their carrot noses is not allowed.
N ever forget to build a snowman!

Emaan Karim (8)
Christ Church CE Primary School, Birmingham

I Love Winter!

I love winter,
It's very cold.
It's Christmas and I always play in the snow.
It's not very warm,
Jesus was born.
It's when Santa comes in red
And you snuggle up in bed.
Christmas is where you play with your friend,
Sadly it ends.

Suheila Arten (8)
Christ Church CE Primary School, Birmingham

Winter

W inter is super cold.
I love the snow, it's so fun.
N ice hot chocolate. I eat it and it's done.
T he day I always do my hairstyle as a bun.
E aster is nice but winter is fun.
R unning around, say bye to the sun.

Yasmeen Saleh (8)
Christ Church CE Primary School, Birmingham

Winter Gives

W inter brings happiness and joy all around.
I t gives us a beautiful sound.
N ight and day we all celebrate.
T ime to be with family.
E nd the day with fun.
R un around in the snow, it's fun for everyone.

Aleesa Maryam (9)
Christ Church CE Primary School, Birmingham

Winter

W inter gives us happiness and joy all around,
I t gives us a lovely sound.
N ice, warm hot chocolate in my belly,
T aking off lots of layers.
E veryone throwing balls,
R unning around knocking on doors.

Haytham Abdorahman (8)
Christ Church CE Primary School, Birmingham

Winter

I love winter!
Winter is cold.
It's when you go on hills with a sleigh
While you are saying, 'Yeah!'
Snowflakes come down while you skate on lakes.
It's when you snuggle up in your bed
While Santa Claus comes in red.

Saba Saghir (9)
Christ Church CE Primary School, Birmingham

Winter's Fun

W inter is full of cold and snow.
I love to play snowball fights.
N ice, hot, yummy hot chocolate in my tummy.
T alking about lots of snowballs.
E veryone is loving it a lot.
R eady for snow to come.

Sumayyah Mahbub (9)
Christ Church CE Primary School, Birmingham

About Winter

W inter is fun because snow comes and it's cold.
I love snow and winter.
N ice cold winter.
T aking all of the snow.
E veryone likes playing snow fights.
R unning around the ice.

Adam Khan (8)
Christ Church CE Primary School, Birmingham

I Love Winter

W inter is cold.
I t's nice to play when it's snowing.
N ever not play in snow.
T elling everyone to play with snow.
E veryone is having fun.
R unning around in the snow.

Muath Hunaiber (8)
Christ Church CE Primary School, Birmingham

Winter

W inter is full of cold.
I remember the hot chocolate that I sold.
N ice raindrops in the air.
T rees of some lovely pears.
E veryone is having fun.
R eptiles chill in the sun.

Maariyah Nadim (8)
Christ Church CE Primary School, Birmingham

Winter

W inter is here and snow is falling
I t's fun playing in the snow
N ice, comfy and having hot chocolate
T rying to keep warm
E veryone is freezing cold
R eady for snow.

Zheer Omer (8)
Christ Church CE Primary School, Birmingham

Winter

W inter is ice-cold with snow.
I ce is everywhere.
N ice hot chocolate down the hatch.
T aking off hats and scarves.
E very day is cold and icy.
R eady to play in the snow.

Rahmah Mohammed (8)
Christ Church CE Primary School, Birmingham

Winter

W inter is for everyone.
I n a warm time with cosy clothes.
N ight and day with families.
T ake off layers.
E nds with a lovely time.
R un around with friends and family.

Fatima Jamil (9)
Christ Church CE Primary School, Birmingham

Winter

Wind vanishing like an earthquake.
Icy snow melting in the bright sun.
Nice hot chocolate in my tummy.
Incredible snowflakes.
Every day it's windy.
Running on the ice. 'Oops, I fell!'

Najma Suleiman (9)
Christ Church CE Primary School, Birmingham

Winter Is Cold

W inter is cold.
I love to play with snowballs.
N ice hot milk in my house.
T aking snow inside.
E veryone playing on skates.
R eady for winter!

Abdul Rahim (8)
Christ Church CE Primary School, Birmingham

Winter

W inter is very frozen.
I love messing about.
N ice hot tea.
T aking lots of layers off.
E veryone is having fun.
R unning around.

Sulaiman Khan (9)
Christ Church CE Primary School, Birmingham

Winter

W ind is so cold.
I am so cold.
N ice snow to play with.
T aking a snowball.
E veryone loves snow.
R emember not to get too cold.

Laraib Akram (8)
Christ Church CE Primary School, Birmingham

Winter

W inter is full of cold.
I ce all around.
N ice warm coffee.
T aking off lots of layers.
E ating noodles.
R unning on the ice.

Kitty Kaur (8)
Christ Church CE Primary School, Birmingham

I Love Winter

I love winter!
Winter is cold.
It's Christmas Day.
It's warm and cold.
I love playing snow fights.
Winter is fun!

Hassan Arshad Hassanili Khan (9)
Christ Church CE Primary School, Birmingham

Untitled

I love winter!
Winter is cold.
It's Christmas Day.
It's warm and cold.
I love playing snow fights.
Winter is fun!

Maleeha Rashid (8)
Christ Church CE Primary School, Birmingham

The Shadow Snow Beast

It is a foggy day,
It is really foggy,
The fog has stopped,
The family ox is gone.
Will it be the shadow snow beast?
The shadow beast can hunt like a wolf.
It can hunt with a fog attack.
There is another fog attack,
I can't see anything!
Am fainting, my eyes are closing,
The shadow snow beast is hiding in the trees,
It grabs me and it is eating me.
I get eaten by the shadow snow beast.

Runnel Hilarion (12)
Highshore School

Untitled

The winter is freezing
Leaves are on the ground.
The ground is white and grey.
The weather is chilly.
People need to wear a hat, scarf, pullover,
Gloves and a jacket.
They eat soup in winter.
They have stew for their lunch.
Some people have fireworks
And they celebrate Christmas.
They play different songs
And sing some carols in the afternoon.
They eat Christmas food at home every Christmas.

Baffour Bediako
Highshore School

The Cold Night

The snow ice-cold, the ice is hard.
On a cold day people drink hot tea.
Do I drink cold tea? you ask.
Yes I do and I love it.
I like it warm so I keep warm
Yet I don't like it when it is too hot
Because it burns my lips.

Icicles are on bicycles.
Snowmen are coming.

Charcoal is on the fire.
On the fire are logs.
Let the fire get bigger.
Do you like the fire?

Bradley Fenn
Highshore School

The Winter Poem

In winter it gets really cold and freezing.
Unfortunately we freeze and shiver.
We need a nice hot cup of tea.
Desperately like a nice, hot, cooked roast dinner.
We have to wear a hat and scarf.
Gloves to keep us warm and cosy.
We all love winter because we do not need to go to school when it is snowing.
Sadly the cars are spoiling our fun and playtime.

Josiah Ferguson (16)
Highshore School

A Cold Wintry Day

On a cold, wintry day
It snowed and snowed and snowed.

It got heavier and heavier
Until Caroline was buried underneath it.

It got colder and colder and colder
Until Caroline froze to death.

When the sun rose everything melted
And no one was there.

Surrounded in silence.

Caroline Jacobs (13)
Highshore School

Christmas Is Coming

Christmas is coming
And December is here.
Santa is coming
With his reindeer.

And the Christmas tree
Is full of presents.
And Christmas joy
And Christmas singing
Are all around us.

Christmas is a good time of year.
A new month
Full of happiness and cheer.

Victor Adeniyi (18)
Highshore School

The Snow Poem

Today we woke up to a snow day
We went to have breakfast
And we went outside in the snow
With friends and family.

We built a snowman together
It was fun and it was cold
So we went in the house to get warm
And to have hot chocolate
It was wonderful.

Rebecca Legood
Highshore School

Winter

Now it's cold out there
It's that time of year.

The snow is falling down.
The leaves are turning brown.

It's Christmas time.
Family put up the tree
With a star for all to see.

It's Christmas time.

Takudzwa Masamba (12)
Highshore School

Winter

The winter is so very cold
The year is getting old
The nights are drawing in
And puddles turn to ice.

The trees have lost their leaves
The geese have flown away
Christmas is getting near
Time for Christmas cheer.

Harry Lorraine-Grimes (12)
Highshore School

Winter

When you are outside
It is cold.
You need to wear your coat and scarf.
At home I have a fire
To keep you warm.
It snows a lot
And I can build a snowman
With a carrot for a nose.
I feel happy.
Winter is fun.

Lilli Stockham (11)
Highshore School

The Winter Storm

It is cold
And dark
And stormy.
I'll go outside
To face the storm.
The wind is loud and powerful.
I put my coat on
To keep me warm and dry.
I feel brave.
I will stop the storm.

David Pearson (12)
Highshore School

Christmas Changes Everywhere

As swallows migrate south
Frost settles on the moor
Snow hares come out of hiding
And leap lightly across the winding hills.

In the pine forest, trees stand close
Whispering secrets for everyone to hear
The thicket lying on the ground
Is cold and sharp underfoot.

The wood that used to be abundant with life
Is now providing no warmth or shelter
Leaving woodland animals to burrow underground
For a place that will hide them from the cold air
That penetrates the land above.

Rivers that used to be flowing
Have now frozen in their tracks
Leaving fish to shiver and cower in the depths
Rocks that used to provide a safe path
Are now slippery with ice.

Prey huddle together hiding from the cold
While predators hunt for a morsel to eat
Christmas changes everywhere.

Frankie Durham (10)
Holy Trinity CE Primary & Nursery School, Richmond

Wintertime Has Come

Winter, winter, what a lovely season to have fun,
Have fun at Christmas with snowballs and snow
And when Christmas trees glow.
The robins chirp, chirp, chirp
And calm carollers sing.
Santa in the sleigh giving generous presents
To children along the way.
Winter wonderland, a place where there is snow and joy.
Hot chocolate and snuggling up by the fire,
Just me and Mum alone.

Salma Mohamed Abdelbaky (9)
Holy Trinity CE Primary & Nursery School, Richmond

Winter Wonderland

Snowflakes fall down onto a transformed world,
Icicles hanging off gutters, sparkling in the morning sunlight.
A robin chirps somewhere in a snow-covered tree.
The village looks like a Christmas card.
Snowball fights are breaking out here and there,
A thin carpet of snow covers houses and roads alike.
I love winter with its beauty and festivals, don't you?

Georgia Allbut (9)
Holy Trinity CE Primary & Nursery School, Richmond

Wintertime

Winter is finally here,
Full of people who cheer.
Everyone has red cheeks and red noses,
That means no good for roses.
It's freezing, frosty and white,
Santa is coming at midnight.
Animals hibernate all happy and warm,
Maybe there will be a big snowstorm.
Some people love winter and some don't,
Will Santa come or maybe he won't!

Alek Pniewski (9)
Holy Trinity CE Primary & Nursery School, Richmond

Winter Is Here!

Snowflakes falling from the sky,
Icicles melting, rising high.
Cinnamon spices, hot chocolate too!
Winter wonderland, festivals,
Something to do!
Then there's church, time to have joy!
Light some calming candles,
Then play with your new toy.
When it's over, don't hurry!
New Year, it's here, don't worry!

Maddy McGeoch (10)
Holy Trinity CE Primary & Nursery School, Richmond

Untitled

Everybody's happy, so we're humming
As snowballs leap into the whirling wind
The animals start migrating and hibernating
The turkey comes out of the oven
And the fire gets lit
When you sit down to open your presents
You find out your granny has knitted for you.
What is special to you about winter?

James Howe (10)
Holy Trinity CE Primary & Nursery School, Richmond

Fox

I creep through the snow
Dragging autumn leaves
Into the burrow
Curling up
Feeling warm
Hearing ravens cackling nearby
The swans flying up above
Mice scratching underneath
Closing my eyes
Waiting for sleep to wash over me
Like a deep, swirling wave.

Panka Eszenyi (9)
Holy Trinity CE Primary & Nursery School, Richmond

Snowman Life

Snowflakes falling from Heaven's hand,
While the blizzard howls,
Since the snow is chilling to the bone,
It will awake all the owls.

Children will go outside,
Because they want to snowball their nan,
Although they mostly want to build
A fantastic snowman.

Snowmen are so lonely,
They are frozen in time,
While watching children play,
But then they melt because of the sun's bright shine.

Until next winter,
When snow starts to fall,
People will build snowmen hyper fast,
Then boot them with a football.

Now you know snowmen's lives,
But hey, you never know
If a snowman
Could fly away to Pluto which is microscopic like an ant.

Gierome Ezekiel Inguito Tinga (8)
Oakridge Junior School, Basingstoke

Little Ol' Snowman

The whole season long,
Snowmen are still,
Singing a song.

'Oh my goodness!'
Says the old mare,
As the little ol' snowman,
Gives him a scare!

Little kids watching 'Danger in da Manger',
While the little ol' snowman,
Starin' at a stranger.

'My, my!'
Says the little white guy,
Because the kid lied,
How sly!

Never mind,
Thought the ol' snowman,
As he overacted.

He saw a ghastly face,
Right in front of him,
So the little ol' snowman,
Tried increasing his pace.

The little ol' snowman,
Was as grim as a poor guy,
Trying to walk,
He was very sly...

Aarib Mohammed (8)
Oakridge Junior School, Basingstoke

Winter's Day

W inter is coming as the sun is fading,
I ce is appearing everywhere!
N otice how the winter came so quickly!
T he bunched-up snow blankets falling gently,
E nding autumn as the cold, fresh air comes.
R ivers turning to ice as people walk and skate over the
S lipping, sliding river.

D o you see the pretty cold snowflakes shooting across the foggy sky and landing ever so gently on your cold face!
A mong all of the soft blankets of snow, there is a very freezing cold ground!
Y ou will see all of the blankets of snow as soon as you walk out of your front door!

Bethany Binder Gharu (9)
Oakridge Junior School, Basingstoke

Winter Is Merry

W onderful sleighing
I n the snow that will freeze your bottom off
N o sad faces, only happy faces
T rees covered in snow in winter
E very snowman has a carrot nose
R eindeer wanting to eat it

I n the snow
S now falling, blanketing the Earth

M erry Christmas to all
E ach winter your bottom gets cold
R are snowflakes drifting to the ground
R eally big piles of snow
Y ou are happy in wonderful winter.

Ben Cameron (8)
Oakridge Junior School, Basingstoke

Winter Rapping Poem

The snow crunching down under your feet while you're marching down the street.
Looking down at the water makes you see your reflection.
The towering trees make you wheeze if you have asthma. I think I just sneezed.
I'm on a mountain, king of the hill, you can't come up because you can't pay your bills.
What's the point of making a snowman if it's going to melt, I shouldn't have kept it on the shelf.
Snowmen are still as statues. If you were one, it would be easy to catch you.

Deshane Hemmings (9)
Oakridge Junior School, Basingstoke

Pine Trees!

When snow falls down,
On pine trees,
With a beautiful fragrance so rare,
Taking me through a world of my own...
I don't know how I could imagine this.

It was a dream with snow everywhere I look,
So beautiful, I run around.
In the distance I see a pine tree.
I run over, I see decorations,
Then decorate the tree so elegant.

I wake up and it was all a dream.
Wishing it could be true.
Seeing it snowing outside,
Could it be true?

Kyla Howlett (9)
Oakridge Junior School, Basingstoke

Snowflake

S now you can throw
N oses that can glow
O rnaments made by a pro
W indows decorated in winter snow make me feel like I want to go
F alling snow falls along the frosty land, let's go
L onely ice sitting on the side melting away time by time
A way the snow goes, but the grass still grows
K ids still playing on the lawn while mowing corn by corn
E ven though winter is over, we will still love our babies being born.

Ruby Bailey McCarthy (9)
Oakridge Junior School, Basingstoke

Frosty Day

F reezing cold air that freezes your face.
R eindeer are seen, even though it's not Christmas.
O ld and classic frost comes back to greet us.
S carily cold and sparkling.
T all trees with crisp leaves dangling down.
Y ou are freezing and sneezing.

D id you need a hot drink?
A nimated people say how sparkly it is.
Y ou go inside, get a hot drink and sit down to rest!

Sasha Suzanne Joyce Petchey (9)
Oakridge Junior School, Basingstoke

Christmas Joy

C is for crackers hanging on the tree.
H is for holly, prickly and green
R is for reindeer with a bright red nose.
I is for icicles and glistening snow.
S is for Santa, a jolly old man.
T is for twinkling lights that hang.
M is for mistletoe, hang it up high.
A is for all of us here, side by side.
S is for stockings hung on our beds, time to go to sleep and rest our little heads.

Felicity Hepden-Barker (9)
Oakridge Junior School, Basingstoke

Waterfall

W inter feels like it never ends
A llowing all snow parts to drop into a waterfall
T eaching nearby the waterfall
E very child likes to swim but not in cold water
R eindeer jumping over the shimmering waterfall
F looding everywhere to be seen in space
A mazing things can happen if you just imagine
L aughing with fish but can't be seen
L onely like snowmen by themselves.

Rhiannon Dixon (9)
Oakridge Junior School, Basingstoke

The Winter Poem

S now is always in winter.
N otice the pretty snow that is as cold as ice.
O ften, the snowflakes tickle your face like feathers.
W eak snow like crusty leaves.
F rost so shiny like glitter.
L eaves on the ground like crisps.
A s cold as a river.
K eep warm clothing on as it is winter.
E asy and soft snow like the middle of a whiteboard.
S now is as fun as JJS.

Erin Langford (8)
Oakridge Junior School, Basingstoke

Christmas

- **C** is for carols that get sung.
- **H** is for holly all around.
- **R** is for reindeer that pull Santa's sleigh.
- **I** is for ice that covers trees.
- **S** is for snowmen that get made by kids.
- **T** is for trees that look pretty.
- **M** is for mistletoe, hang it up high, you might get a kiss as someone walks by.
- **A** is for antlers on reindeer.
- **S** is for snow on Santa's sleigh.

Jacob-Joshua Agozzino (8)
Oakridge Junior School, Basingstoke

Pretty Snowflakes

Snowflakes, snowflakes pretty and light,
How on earth are they so bright?
Shiny snowflakes wake up now,
Let's go and have some fun now!
Sparkly snowflakes come down now,
Just see how they sparkle down!
Snowflakes spread when you see,
Why don't we let them free?
Beautiful snowflakes shimmer down,
Always like a frosty kite!
Snowflakes, snowflakes, come on now,
How are you silver-white?

Nivedha Sudhakaran (8)
Oakridge Junior School, Basingstoke

Snowflakes

S ymmetrical snowflakes falling from above,
N ewly laid snow on the ground,
O ne snowflake is never the same
W inter is when they often come
F rost on your windowpane
L ighter than a feather
A fter they fall, they cover the rooftops of houses,
K ick the silver-white snow as you walk
E yelashes covered with snow
S wirling down onto the grass.

Mollie Lovick (9)
Oakridge Junior School, Basingstoke

Snowflakes

S now bomb as it hits the ground
N on-stop falling
O nly ends when the sun comes out
W atery as they melt
F lying down and tickles your nose
L ike a tap when they melt
A s it falls, it feels good when they touch your nose
K icking the snow makes more snowflakes
E ndless snowflakes drop
S o many trees covered with snowflakes.

Samuel Ackland (9)
Oakridge Junior School, Basingstoke

Winter Poem

S ilver snowman glittering in the beautiful moonlight.
N otice how the snowmen melt in the bright sunshine.
O ften, the snowmen melt so quickly that we feel sorry for them.
W e have so much fun building the snowmen.
M elt if you turn them in the dazzling fire
A nd they look so pretty when they're finished.
N ever take them indoors or they will melt.

Alexandra Kalashnikova (8)
Oakridge Junior School, Basingstoke

Frosty Days

F rost covers trees like a blanket
R obins have red breasts, only colour you see
O ne snowflake, never the same
S waying so merrily
T ickled by snow
Y ew trees covered

D ays look like nights
A brilliant sight for my eyes!
Y ou can always enjoy frosty days
S oothing and calm as every day should be.

Fida Salam (9)
Oakridge Junior School, Basingstoke

Wintertime At Heart

Lakes as solid as frozen ice.
Sleet as soggy as the horrible rain.
Leaves as crunchy as cornflakes being eaten quickly.
Snow as soft as a kitten.
Trees as bare as can be.
Snowflakes as symmetrical as a square.
The sky is as silver-white as plain paper.
Robins chirping loudly like a monkey.
Frost glimmering like the stars.
Fresh breeze as nippy as the freezer.

Adonia Bala (9)
Oakridge Junior School, Basingstoke

Snowmen Poem

S now-covered hills glistening so bright
N ippy breeze fills the silent air
O ften you see the snow in the early morning
W indowpane is always pearly with the glass so glittery
M elting snow covered the beautiful earth
E njoy sleighing down a glittering hill
N oisy night so you can't sleep because you're so excited.

Rosie Livingstone (8)
Oakridge Junior School, Basingstoke

Wintertime

In winter, I love
Silver-white frost like glitter on the ground,
Snow as soft as kitten's fur,
Frozen leaves on the ground like crisps,
Icicles as sharp as a knife,
Ice as cold as new ice cream,
Pearly snow as white as doves,
Crystal-clear icicles as sharp as daggers,
Snowflakes falling down like feathers,
Biting wind as cold as ice.

Malak Oisti (9)
Oakridge Junior School, Basingstoke

Wonderful Winter

Oh lake, oh lake
How cold you are
Your temperature
Is quite bizarre.

The trees around you
Stretch so high
They almost reach
Into the sky.

Oh sky, oh sky
How blue you look
When you are drawn
Into a book.

When you cross the bridge
Tomorrow
Do not leave the bridge
In sorrow.

Robert Allwright (8)
Oakridge Junior School, Basingstoke

Christmas Poem

C andles shining as bright as the sun
H olly as red as blood
R oses to give to your bride
I cicles stuck together when you skate
S wimming in very cold water
T ree branches falling down
M ake do with what you have
A s cold as climbing a mountain
S hining stars in the night.

Ella-Mae Stent (8)
Oakridge Junior School, Basingstoke

Winter

W et floor, but only when the snow melts
I nteresting snowflakes falling when you're fast asleep
N ice crystal in the sparkling snowflakes
T ouches us with the sparkling snow which looks amazing
E arth covered in snow which is as white as paper
R ouge cheeks, feeling hot but cold to touch.

Jack Williams (8)
Oakridge Junior School, Basingstoke

Winter Days

Notice the winter snow outside,
Where it does reside.
You feel the winter that is bitter
And see the snow like glitter.
Feel the raw and chilly air
And enjoy the frost that is rare.
But it will not stay,
Soon it will decay.
In February and in late spring,
Soon in three months it will be dying,
Be dying.

Sreeram Suresh Setlur (8)
Oakridge Junior School, Basingstoke

Snowman Poem

S is for snow covering the ground.
N is for Noel.
O is for on his own waiting for someone to play with him.
W is for wishing to be in a freezing cold castle.
M is for mate that the snowman needed.
A is for awesome toys under the tree.
N is for never to be seen the same way again.

Ollie Cowton (8)
Oakridge Junior School, Basingstoke

Snowflakes

S now you can throw.
N oel is Christmas.
O rnaments on Christmas trees.
W inter wonderland.
F rosty snow on trees.
L eaves fall off trees.
A ngels are like butterflies.
K ris Kringle is Santa.
E vergreen leaves.
S nowflakes fall from the sky.

Kia Crawford-Hicks (9)
Oakridge Junior School, Basingstoke

A Miracle Of Winter!

Winter is a miracle for some
But a miracle for some
Some say it's magic
They even have a laugh
When snow falls

If you're in a muddle
Or have some trouble
Be sure to jump in a puddle

If chocolate is the case
Go to a place
Where you can buy some snowflakes.

Isabelle Pauline Pike (9)
Oakridge Junior School, Basingstoke

Love Winter

S now and frost everywhere
N othing is warm enough
O verpowered snowball throwers out practising
W inter wonderland
B abies hibernating
A ll are having fun
L ove the snow the whole season long
L ove it while you still can
S pread the word.

Adam Grant (8)
Oakridge Junior School, Basingstoke

Winter

W hite snow like confetti falling to the ground
I cicles like daggers hang from the roof
N ice and cosy by the warm fire
T rees with the leaves all gone
E xcept the evergreens with their lovely colour
R eindeer come every Christmas Eve night in the glistening snow.

Poppy Williams (8)
Oakridge Junior School, Basingstoke

Merry

M istletoe hung up high as you may get a kiss as someone walks by
E xtraordinary pie is just right for a lad like Santa
R ed berries on a holly leaf may get you to sleep
R udolph so bright you could see him walking by
Y ule logs keep you warm while there is a winter storm.

Cindy Tafrey (9)
Oakridge Junior School, Basingstoke

Wintertime Poem

S ilky, white snow covered everything
N ight and day children laugh and play
O rnaments frosty like a snowman
W inter cold breezes blowing the trees
M istletoe hanging
A lot of children built a snowman
N ice, caring children playing in the snow.

Charlotte Hazel Fry (8)
Oakridge Junior School, Basingstoke

Christmas

Christmas only comes once a year
So bring the happiness with a cheer
Lots of lovely food we get
We eat with no regret

Presents are under the Christmas tree
One for you, two for me
Twinkling lights too bright for my eyes
Shut them tight and dream of mince pies.

Harris Waheed (8)
Oakridge Junior School, Basingstoke

Winter

Snowflakes falling like paper swaying side to side
Icicles as sharp as knives falling and digging into the ground
Dark grey days as they turn into nights
Days get shorter, nights get longer
Snowballs as big as boulders rolling around on a field
Ice as slippery as a wooden floor.

Ronnie Tuffs (8)
Oakridge Junior School, Basingstoke

The Fun Of Winter

Winter is here
Now that the snow has arrived
The fields are a white blanket
The ice is as slippery as a wet, wooden floor
Snowballs and sledging are here
It is as cold as the bottom of the sea
The frost on the windows are like snowflakes
The winter is fun.

Sam Thorpe (8)
Oakridge Junior School, Basingstoke

Winter Poem

In winter I love,
Clear ice as clean as crystals over lakes and windows.
Snow falls down like a piece of paper.
Leaves crunch like crisps.
Winter is as cold as space without a space suit.
Air is as fresh as water is around.
Snowballs are thrown like frisbees in the air.

Cameron Reeve (8)
Oakridge Junior School, Basingstoke

Winter

W inter, sparkly snow when winter is near
I ce snow as cold as a freezer
N otice when you wake up it is all white
T rees are covered with white blankets of snow
E arth covered in snow everywhere
R ivers running under the ice of snow.

Loren Carter (8)
Oakridge Junior School, Basingstoke

Wintertime Rhyme

W indy it is, in wintertime
I cicles as sharp as knives that hang down
N ight looks like it's all the time
T ickly snowflakes everywhere I go
E xcellent, gorgeous, calm, it is sparkling ice
R obins are as red as holly berries.

Marnie Clarkson (9)
Oakridge Junior School, Basingstoke

Winter

W hat a wonderful snow
I cicles are hanging in the beautiful caves
N owhere does the sun come in the snowy lands
T ress will be bare now
E ndless snowflakes come all over the land
R unning through the snow there were snow ploughs.

Krishna Volety (8)
Oakridge Junior School, Basingstoke

Snowmen

S nowmen are built by you,
N ose is orange like a carrot,
O h no, you can't see them because they blend in,
W hite as a cloud,
M elt as quickly as the wind,
E yes made from coal,
N ever come to life!

Rose Mason (8)
Oakridge Junior School, Basingstoke

Wintertime

W indy day making branches sway.
I nside there is a fire crackling.
N umb hands and frozen feet.
T ingling fingers when you get warm.
E ating turkey while watching the evening glow.
R unning around in pearly snow.

Misha Sirnani (8)
Oakridge Junior School, Basingstoke

Frosty Days

In winter I love,
Snowflakes as cold as a fridge.
Snow like crunchy micro leaves,
Snowballs like extreme ice.
Icicles like sharp, pointy, shark's teeth.
Snowballs like an ice rink,
Frost like a water fountain.

Jacob Newson (9)
Oakridge Junior School, Basingstoke

Winter Poem

When you touch ice,
It feels really nice.
When it gets cold,
You feel like you're gold.
When you see snow,
You want it to grow.
When snowflakes float,
You need to wear a coat.

Tyson Mathurin (8)
Oakridge Junior School, Basingstoke

Why I Love Winter

Winter's coming, summer's going,
Like a flash.
Wintry breeze like a fan blowing on you.
Sleet like rain but with snow.
Snowflakes like a blanket covering the ground.

George Chubb (8)
Oakridge Junior School, Basingstoke

Snow, Oh Wonderful Snow!

Snow, oh wonderful snow!
White, glistening snow falling down.
If you're outside then you'll get an icy crown,
Gradually you'll start to see a thick layer of snow,
You can make a snowman and watch him glow.

Snow, oh wonderful snow!
I'm watching your wintry show,
I sit at my window sill watching you fall,
Waiting for my sister's call.

Snow, oh wonderful snow!
'Come on,' she shouts, 'let's go.'
Out in the freezing cold, crunching under my foot,
'Let's make a snowman, with hair of soot.'

Snow, oh wonderful snow!
Shining from the sky in a stormy flow,
Tickling my nose and making it cold.
I will always love the snow even when I'm old!

India Page (9)
Peak Forest CE Primary School, Buxton

The Coming Of Winter

Snowflakes
Filling the air,
Landing on the white, cold carpet,
Turning the glacial ground to stone.
Frozen little robins tweet on the tree branch.
Fickle, delicate leaves lie on the icy, Arctic ground.
Grizzly bears hiding in the snow, giving birth to their cute cubs.
The coming of winter will start all of these.
Trees fixed in the ground, still and towering, stripped of their leaves,
Streams frozen into thick ice,
Frost freezing the leaves,
Snow making green fields white.
This is winter.
As the birds fly away,
As the small creatures hide,
These towns and villages will become forsaken
From all living things.
This is winter.

Callum (10)
Peak Forest CE Primary School, Buxton

Snow

As **S**hiny as a trophy,
Falli**N**g like leaves off a tree,
As c**O**ld as ice,
As **W**hite as paper,
Dazzl**I**ng like diamonds.
Snowme**N** were
Gleaming under the sun.

Ethan White (8)
Peak Forest CE Primary School, Buxton

A Winter Poem

Silver, shining snow,
Settled on the hillside like a white blanket
That you would wrap around yourself when in front of a fire,
Cosy and warm with a cup of hot chocolate.
The snow crackled and crunched under their feet
And froze their blood as the cold air hit their body like icy daggers.
Suddenly, the wind screamed and shot diamonds through the air.
Long, thin swords hung threateningly on the crystallised barn roof as if they were about to fall.
Then chills went down their spine and they knew winter had come!

Grace Kirkham (10)
Peak Forest CE Primary School, Buxton

The Snow

Snow is as cold as a freezer.
It comes in winter.
People get happier, people build snowmen.
People get cold,
People grow colder as the cold scales up their legs.
People get wet.
People slip, people slide and get ice-burn.
Sometimes people get frostbite.
Snow melts in people's eyes, leaving water.
Snow lands on people's tongues.
Cotton wool falls from the sky.
Leaves rain, taking over the streets.

Matthew Jagger (8)
Peak Forest CE Primary School, Buxton

The Snow

All around us like a massive white sheet covering the hills.
It is deeper on the moor.
Flickering crystals fall from above.
The snow lays like a blanket glistening on the ground, sparkling like a Christmas tree.
The icy berries on the tree were like ruby-red Christmas lights.
I am warm and cosy inside,
Watching the snow fall in the clear night sky.

Bethany Hadfield (9)
Peak Forest CE Primary School, Buxton

Winter Hill...

The snow is like a freezer,
The river is dead,
The wind is in a temper,
The trees are owners of a thousand swords.

The sheep are like camouflaged chameleons,
The ruby-red, icy berries resemble Christmas tree lights.
The barn is like an igloo,
The village is a steaming cauldron.

Beatrix (10)
Peak Forest CE Primary School, Buxton

The Snow

It was falling as fast as a shooting star,
It was dancing in the wind like angels,
It was landing in the branches like birds,
It was covering the fields like glitter,
The ice was as tough as concrete,
The cold had frozen the river dead.

James G (8)
Peak Forest CE Primary School, Buxton

The Snow

Snow is bright.
Snow is white.
Snow is light.
Snow might fall tonight.
Snow makes sounds go quiet.
Snow is as bright as a white marshmallow.
Snow is a marshmallow.
Snow waves as it falls.

Oliver (9)
Peak Forest CE Primary School, Buxton

Winter

In winter I found a duck with blood around its neck
It was in the snow.
It tried to swim on the ice
The corn was solid as a brick.
I thought it would die,
But it survived.

Jim Hayes (7)
Peak Forest CE Primary School, Buxton

Winter

The sun was dazzling.
The snow was beautiful.
The fish were frozen under the ice.
The dazzling creatures were shivering in the ice cave.

Maia Fletcher (7)
Peak Forest CE Primary School, Buxton

A Snowy, Wintry Day

I walk out the oak door and underneath my feet,
I hear the crunching of soft snow,
The bright, shining sun still very low,
The snow is falling like flour through a sieve,
Obviously God's gift.

The shimmering Northern Lights,
All our ancestors who took flight,
The lights look like ripples on a river,
The tiny reflection of silver.

In the distance on the nearby hill,
There are cries of laughter
And an ear-piercing shrill,
Children making snow angels and snowmen,
Playing out till ten.

As the day moves on,
The sun is soon gone,
The icy, bitter winds,
Blowing like a whirlwind.

Snowball fights all night,
The blanket of snow, a muddy white,
No snow left to play with tonight,
But today was a great delight.

Time to go home,
Out of the snow-like foam,
Snuggling in the heat,
Drinking a steaming hot chocolate treat.

Michaela Hancock (14)
The Manor Academy, Mansfield

Winter's Christmas

Winter is here,
Everyone cheer!
Squirrels are sleeping,
Willows are weeping,
While the lights illuminate Christmas Day.

Stockings hang,
Crackers bang!
Paper hats worn,
Snow on the lawn,
While the lights illuminate Christmas Day.

Snowmen stand there,
Hats they all wear!
Stars shine so bright,
As they dance through the night,
While the lights illuminate Christmas Day.

Presents are waiting under the tree,
When people see them, they fill up with glee!
Kids love Santa the most,
All the letters for him in the post,
While the lights illuminate Christmas Day.

Joseph and Mary,
On a donkey not hairy!
Jesus came to the world,
In a haystack He curled,

While the lights illuminate Christmas Day.

Frosty breeze blows,
Squawk! say the crows!
Hedgehogs hibernate,
Some people celebrate,
While the lights illuminate Christmas Day.

Christmas long gone,
Winter hangs on!
Snow starts to melt,
Santa loosens his belt,
The lights did illuminate Christmas Day.

Megan Jenkins (11)
Ysgol Gynradd Gymraeg Llantrisant, Pontyclun

Wintertime

Snowflakes falling
Icicles melting
This is wintertime.

Berries falling
Robins flying
This is wintertime.

Hands shivering
Mittens warming
This is wintertime.

Fire glowing
Candles flickering
This is wintertime.

People skating
Twirling, spinning
This is wintertime.

Snowmen freezing
Snowballs landing
This is wintertime.

Lights glistening
Tinsel sparkling
This is wintertime.

Children laughing
Calendars opening
This is wintertime.

Santa travelling
Rudolph guiding
This is wintertime.

One star shining
Three kings following
This is wintertime.

Jesus sleeping
Mary watching
This is wintertime.

Christmas is coming
People celebrating
I love wintertime!

Nia Powell (10)
Ysgol Gynradd Gymraeg Llantrisant, Pontyclun

Christmas In Castle House

Big black gates standing in snowflakes,
Christmas lights covering the courtyard,
Steep, slippery, icy steps,
Swirling branches on bare trees.

The inquisitive squirrel with his bushy tail,
Prickly hedgehogs rushing around,
Sneaky foxes in white dresses,
Bird feeders emptying quickly.

Tomorrow, the sweep comes to clear the chimney,
Bright colours in a dancing fire,
Our family enjoy the feasts and jokes,
My brother and I play and laugh.

The night before Christmas,
Our tree twinkles in a bay window,
We dream about Santa,
Ribbons and wrapping paper everywhere.

Shh, what's that noise?
Bells singing, deer eating,
Watch Santa! Watch your dirty boots,
Presents waiting to be opened.

This Christmas is going to be the best Christmas ever
In our new home!

Hedd Teifi (10)
Ysgol Gynradd Gymraeg Llantrisant, Pontyclun

Winter

It's winter, it's winter
and I've got a cold.
I'm coughing, I'm sneezing,
I'm blowing my nose.
I am trembling from the top of my head
to my toes.
It's winter, it's winter
and I am feeling cold.
The nights are so long
and so short is the day.
I hardly get any time to go out and play.

The Christmas lights are in my sight,
The Christmas trees are up and bright.
Everything about Christmas brings me delight
and I wait for Santa to arrive at night
to bring me something nice and bright.
Everyone wakes up with joy in their heart,
waiting for the festivities to start.

Harley Rose Vigliotta (11)
Ysgol Gynradd Gymraeg Llantrisant, Pontyclun

White Snow

Children looking out of their windows,
They see something white outside, not bird feathers,
Actual snow! They celebrate like they've won £1,000,
Parents not so happy to see, but let them play.

Sleds rushing quickly down the hills,
Snowman with a pointy carrot on his nose,
Instead of football, we have snowball fights
And people not so happy have hot chocolate with sprinkles.

When the winter ends, the snow is melting,
School is starting, children moaning,
Happy parents having late night parties with friends,
And that's what normally happens in winter.

Llewelyn Gwynne (10)
Ysgol Gynradd Gymraeg Llantrisant, Pontyclun

Christmas Eve

The night before Christmas
Excitedly going to bed,
All I can think about
Is Santa in my head.
I wonder if he's got all the toys
For all the girls
And all the boys.
I hope he's got my letter,
To make my wishes better.
Meanwhile I look up at the sky
And there he is passing by!
I go back to sleeping
And pretend not to be peeping.
Hoping the morning will arrive soon,
Then I'll be over the moon!
Opening all my presents from under the tree,
With all my family
And me!

Emily Lauren Gait (10)
Ysgol Gynradd Gymraeg Llantrisant, Pontyclun

Winter Wonderland

In winter there is lots of snow
The stars in the sky will brightly glow,
We wrap up warm, with hats and gloves,
We think about the ones we love.

The three men who visit Jesus are wise,
They bring a lovely big surprise,
We now give presents, from Santa too,
All around the world, we say thank you!

Santa goes, 'Ho, ho, ho!'
On his sleigh with special cargo,
Holly and ivy in wreaths with red berries,
We hope your Christmas is very merry.

Emily Harris (9)
Ysgol Gynradd Gymraeg Llantrisant, Pontyclun

The Perfect Christmas

Hanging ornaments like baubles and holly,
Having a fun time and feeling jolly.
With beautiful snow,
And ornaments that glow,
Receiving greetings,
Robins giving tweetings.

Stars shining bright,
In the night.
Sweet tasting berries,
Feeling very merry.
Presents and gifts
As the snow drifts.

Winter, Christmas every year,
Tinsel and baubles,
We'll celebrate with cheer.

Grace Morgan (9)
Ysgol Gynradd Gymraeg Llantrisant, Pontyclun

Last Christmas

Last Christmas I stole your heart,
But all your memories helped you a lot
And all your dreams were on a little cart
And everyone has a memorable Christmas.

On Christmas Eve you cry
Because Santa is coming,
But all you want to do is buy,
Everyone likes it when you really behave, don't they?

He carries a huge sack,
Full of presents and toys
On his back
And eats a little mince pie.

Mali Foster (9)
Ysgol Gynradd Gymraeg Llantrisant, Pontyclun

Christmas Joy

'Tis the season to be jolly,
Children playing in the snow,
Little robin in the holly,
Putting on a Christmas show.

Baby Jesus in the manger,
Cattle lowing all around,
Unaware of Herod's danger,
Many presents on the ground.

Mary looking down at her child,
Children hoping St Nick will come,
Santa ate a mince pie and smiled,
At Christmas no one should be glum.

Mali Stevenson (10)
Ysgol Gynradd Gymraeg Llantrisant, Pontyclun

Snowy Fun Time

Having fun in the snow
Watching robins flying low
Building snowmen in the garden
But in snowstorms they are hidden.

Skating on the crystal lake
This is fun, no mistake
Sledging down a slippery slope
Holding tightly to the rope.

Fun and laughter with my friends
I hope this fun never ends
Flakes are falling on my head
It's nearly time for my bed.

Owain Prys Ifans Jones (9)
Ysgol Gynradd Gymraeg Llantrisant, Pontyclun

Winter!

A time for cuddling our loved ones by a warm fire,
A time for eating mince pies and turkey,
A time for catching up with friends and family,
A time for finding that special gift to make someone smile,
A time for wrapping up warm on cold winter days,
A time for decorating your Christmas tree,
A time for counting down the days until Santa arrives,
A time for love...
Winter!

Cerys Hulse (11)
Ysgol Gynradd Gymraeg Llantrisant, Pontyclun

This Winter

I would like to keep warm this winter
Keep inside from the cold and maybe snow
I'll decorate my cards with glitter
While watching the evening glow.

I will also be celebrating Christmas this year
With decorations around the place
Ringing bells are what I want to hear
And there will be children with smiles on their faces.

Benjamin Samuel Williams (10)
Ysgol Gynradd Gymraeg Llantrisant, Pontyclun

This Winter Time

The stars are shining
On a cold, frosty night
And the moonlight shines across the ice,
All twinkling and sparkling, what a sight!

The children are dreaming about Christmas Day,
What presents Santa has wrapped up on his sleigh.
The exciting sound of the sleigh bells they hear,
What a wonderful time winter is this year.

Owain John (11)
Ysgol Gynradd Gymraeg Llantrisant, Pontyclun

A Wintry Night

The sky is dark and the ground is white.
The world is peaceful on this wintry night.
There is not a thing in sight,
Not even a bird taking flight.
It's just me and the snow this wintry night.
I love the snow,
I just don't want it to go.
I love winter the way it is,
I don't want it to change a single bit.

Elis Burton (11)
Ysgol Gynradd Gymraeg Llantrisant, Pontyclun

Christmas

The snow glistens upon the ground,
Snowflakes falling all around.

Carol singers knocking door to door,
People asking for some more.

Don't forget the carrots and mince pie,
For Santa flying through the sky.

Christmas Day is here at last,
It's time to open presents fast.

Lili Hopkins (10)
Ysgol Gynradd Gymraeg Llantrisant, Pontyclun

Christmas Time!

I will remember my childhood days,
In lots and lots of different ways,
With fairy tales and Christmas lights
And lots and lots of snowball fights.

Playing carols, the wrapping is done,
No more shopping for anyone.
Putting up the tree and having fun,
it's such a special time for everyone...!

Emily Amos (10)
Ysgol Gynradd Gymraeg Llantrisant, Pontyclun

Winter Fun Has Won!

In winter, lots of snow falls down
The magic of Christmas arrives in town
Lots of families having fun
Boring loses and the winter has won

The Christmas tree shines so bright
Spreading Christmas spirit through the night
Wrapping the tinsel all around
Is what makes Christmas so much fun.

Sam Jones (10)
Ysgol Gynradd Gymraeg Llantrisant, Pontyclun

I Love Christmas!

When the snow blows
And the weather gets colder,
The lights of Christmas are shining like stars.
Bells are jingling happily,
The snowmen are dancing cheerfully,
The trees are blowing wildly,
People are singing Christmas carols amazingly!

Rhys Morgan Stephens (10)
Ysgol Gynradd Gymraeg Llantrisant, Pontyclun

Untitled

The tree is green,
The tinsel is gold,
The baubles are red
And the colours of the rainbow.

The presents are wrapped,
With a big bow,
Hilarious cards with a smile,
Christmas cheer, Santa is here.

Lois James (9)
Ysgol Gynradd Gymraeg Llantrisant, Pontyclun

Wintertime!

The sparkling lights on the Christmas tree,
Make me happy and cheery.
We wrap up warm against the north wind,
Icy blizzards so strong and cold,
Cosy fires to welcome us home,
Steaming hot soup to make us warm!

Charlotte Simcock (10)
Ysgol Gynradd Gymraeg Llantrisant, Pontyclun

Wintry Rhymes

Snow, white and soft
Cold, shivering and shaking
Christmas presents and fun.

January, long and miserable
Frosty, crisp and freezing
But, I love the cold winter.

Jac Lloyd Lockett (10)
Ysgol Gynradd Gymraeg Llantrisant, Pontyclun

Young Writers Information

We hope you have enjoyed reading this book – and that you will continue to in the coming years.

If you're a young adult who enjoys reading and creative writing, or the parent of an enthusiastic poet or story writer, do visit our website **www.youngwriters.co.uk**. Here you will find free competitions, workshops and games, as well as recommended reads, a poetry glossary and our blog.

If you would like to order further copies of this book, or any of our other titles, then please give us a call or visit **www.youngwriters.co.uk**.

Young Writers
Remus House
Coltsfoot Drive
Peterborough
PE2 9BF
(01733) 890066
info@youngwriters.co.uk